"the desire of My heart"

God's Word for Our Time

by

Richard Hobbs

By the same author
"A MORE PERFECT WAY" -
Meditations on the Stations of the Cross
published by Anthony Clarke Publications,
Wheathampstead, Herts

Published by Mrs. E.K. Hobbs
ISBN 0 9525306 0 0
Copyright © 1995 Elise Hobbs
No part of this publication may be reproduced or transmitted, in any form
or by any means, electronic, mechanical, photocopying, recording or
otherwise, or stored in any retrieval system of any nature, without written
permission.

Designed by The Blackthorn Group, P.O. Box 41,
Wallingford OX10 6TD   01491-641044
Printed by Caric Press   01264 354887

RICHARD HOBBS - FRIEND AND PROPHET
by Charles Whitehead

When I first met Richard Hobbs in the mid-1980s I sensed that the Lord had given him to his people "for such a time as this". It soon became clear that Richard had a very special gift of prophecy, and the Lord began to use him to speak out clearly and powerfully.

His presence, voice, and temperament were well suited to the prophetic ministry.

Richard was a man who prayed and discerned much before speaking, but when he felt the time was right to speak, the message came with clarity and authority. The most common themes were unity and peace, with a concern for the poor, the oppressed and under-privileged, and a constant reminder that we are to be uncomplicated and child-like when it comes to the things of God and His Kingdom.

Despite the authority and effect of the many words he received and faithfully delivered, Richard remained in awe of the ministry he had been given, never taking it for granted or abusing it, but always seeking discernment and reaction lest anything of himself devalue what his Lord wanted to say through him.

I have re-read many of the words he sent me over the years, and whilst I always encouraged him and never doubted the authenticity of his ministry, I have recently come to understand even more fully their importance and accuracy, and I am now challenged afresh as I read some of those I have never seen before. I hope that further selections will be published at a later date.

While most people will remember him as the tall, humble man with the gift of prophecy, I believe that the Lord also used Richard as a great example, and as an encourager. He made the world a richer and better place for all of us, and in this little book he continues to be a willing channel through whom God still speaks to His people. For me, Richard was a prophet of God, a man of integrity, commitment, and vision, but above all, a friend to many. He concluded his own written testimony with these words:

"I am very happy to see myself as working for the Lord, which is a real change from the time when I longed to be rich and powerful and to be the one in charge, and God w… a tough parent who was always judging my efforts. 'I feel like a child, but I know that if I let Him, o… her will lead us where He wants us to go and … ugh the going may be pretty hard at times, it will be good when we get there. I wonder where He will take us over the next few years?"

I think God our Father told us something about where He wants to take us, and how He wants us to live, through the words He gave to Richard. I am delighted to write this foreword and to encourage the reader to dwell deeply upon the messages in the pages that follow.

INTRODUCTION
by Ron Nicholls

For the ten years that Richard was associated with the Alton Day of Renewal, he used faithfully to give me, and other members of the core group, copies of all that he wrote down at the command of the Lord. His was a prophetic ministry in the true sense of the word, exercised, recognised and developed from within an approving community and with obvious fruit.

He frequently said that it was the encouragement and support of the regular attenders at the monthly Days of Renewal which helped him develop that ministry. The humility with which he submitted his words to our core group for discernment was an example to us all and I, as coordinator, frequently felt challenged by the uncompromising things which I heard the Lord saying to me through Richard.

As Richard listened to God in the days preceding our meetings, the themes which the Lord prompted onto his pages were almost invariably confirmed by other members of our core group after their own prayers and Bible readings. Such a powerful sense of oneness in preparation for a public meeting of up to 100 people was, and is, a convincing witness for the building up of the body. c.f. Ephesians 4, 12 & 13. Truly we serve a wonderful Lord ... to Him be all glory ...

CONTENTS

Page

My Body Grows Person By Person	9
Do Not Look Back	10
You Are One Nation Called To Holiness	11
I Call You To Build My Body	12
Whom Do You Obey?	13
The New Life Is Hidden	14
Where The Spirit Is Present ...	15
I Need All To Help	16
Mother Of Unity	17
I Am One God Though Three Persons, Perfect Model Of Unity	18
Are You Like Me?	20
My Mother Is My Perfect Creature	21
My Father Is Tender Hearted	22
The Spirit Blows Where He Wills	23
Friends, Follow Me	24
Your Real Names	25
Rejoice In Your Differences	26
Offer Me	27
I Have Forgiven You	28
Beauty Is From God	30
Give Praise At All Times	31
I Can Share The Pain And The Happiness With You	32
Mother Of Your Unity	33
I Am Reflected In Your Eyes	34
Who Sits At My Table?	35
Make Yourself Vulnerable	36
Dry Bones	37
My Eyes, My Ears	38
Listen To Each Other	39
My Love Has No Conditions	40
Who Stands With Me?	42
Marks Of Love	43

Page

Pride Is Opaque	44
Do Not Cling To Your Past	45
Come Into My Presence	46
The Darkness Of No-peace	47
Accept Your Parentage	48
Remove The Nails So I Can Come Down	49
Listen To My Words	50
My Crown Of Thorns Unites You	51
Children Of The Promise	52
Turn The Other Cheek	54
I Cannot Lie	55
Discernment	55
Come Closer Into My Light	56
Travel Together In A Body	57
You Will Be One In Heaven	58
A Holy Nation Set Apart	59
Competition In Service	60
Accept Insecurity	61
Lift Up Your Eyes	62
Seek Those Who Love My Words	64
I Can Do No More To Persuade You	66
Come! Set Aside Your Differences	68
The Meadows Of Adoration	70

'To God be the Glory'

MY BODY GROWS PERSON BY PERSON

My body is built up of living souls,
not of churches.
Just as I did not come into the world fully grown
but chose to develop, cell by cell,
in my mother's womb,
and then to grow gradually from a baby to a man,
so it is with my body among you on earth.
Unity is not to be achieved
by negotiation between the leaders of the churches,
kings and high priests making treaties
on behalf of the people under their authority.
Unity will be achieved
when two or three humble people
meet together in my name,
and cry out with my mother,
"My soul glorifies the Lord,
who has done great things for me."

My body grows person by person,
just as I grew cell by cell.
All your high level negotiations can do
is to remove obstacles
to the meetings of the poor and humble;
the real growing together in me
happens when you listen to me
and give words of comfort
to those who are weary;
when you share your bread with the hungry,
bind up the wounds of the sick
and give company to the lonely,
all in my name.
Then the world will be filled with my glory,
and I shall be among you again.

DO NOT LOOK BACK

Do not look back.
In the new light of the Resurrection
you will be one,
for I make all things new
each day,
and I forget utterly
the darkness that is past.

Seek me in the freshness of the garden
and kneel at my feet.
You are joined
because you all seek and see me.
No matter that you would describe me
differently,
if asked.
I do not ask you to describe me,
but to love me,
and to do my will.

As long as it is me
that you seek
and at whose feet you kneel,
I AM WHO I AM
and the person for all.
You will all see me differently
because of your different backgrounds,
but in seeing me
you will be seeing the same Lord.

YOU ARE ONE NATION CALLED TO HOLINESS

Trust me
and never think that I am not trustworthy,
even though I am mocked and scourged.
I do not tell you
to seek for tribulation;
but if it comes,
do not doubt that I am with you
and that I have gone before you
on the same road.
Those who saw me scourged in Jerusalem
did not know that after my passion
I would rise again in new life;
but you do.
So be of good heart;
do not lose hope.
I am trustworthy
and I have won the victory.
And whoever trusts me
will inherit the land;
he will own my holy mountain.

I have shown you how you can be one
by bringing you together
from the East and from the West.
No one asked if you were
a Catholic or a Protestant,
but you all praise my name as one body.
There will be pain for you in the future
if you are true to what you have learned.
You will be accused of disloyalty
to your church and even to your country.
But remember that I made you
one living body,
to suffer and to rejoice together.
For you are one nation called to holiness,
my people called to re-present
my passion, death and resurrection to the world
so that the world may believe.

I CALL YOU TO BUILD MY BODY

I made each one of you different,
each nation, each family, each individual,
so that you could form one glorious body,
the body of my only Son.
I made you to complement one another
so that you would all be able to experience
the joy of complete self-giving,
the love that is the very life of your God,
the love of Father for Son,
and of Son for Father,
the Holy Spirit that is their love
for each other.

None of you is able to exist alone;
each of you needs the company and support of others.
Together you can be the image of God among men,
a community of mutual love and tenderness.
How else could you begin to experience my love
other than by experiencing the love of others
and giving them your love in return,
until you are surprised
by the overpowering love of my Spirit,
which comes upon all those
who open their hearts to my will.

Then I am born within you,
and I can grow until you have become
my presence in the world to others;
so that when they look at you
they see only me,
because your eyes are always on me,
your ears listening to me,
and your lips continually saying,
"Do whatever he tells you."

And when you are wholly absorbed in me,
then I will call you into my presence
and I will say to my Father,
"Here is your beloved son,
your beloved daughter.
Let us welcome them into our glory."
And the whole court of heaven rejoices
as each one of my saints
is added to their company,
for their coming adds one more part
to my glorious body,
and brings closer the time
when I will come again on earth
to bring all things to completion.

WHOM DO YOU OBEY?

Whom do you obey?
If I say go,
will you go?
It is a time to prepare
for my coming
and I need all the workers
who are available.
This is the eleventh hour,
and all who have no employer
can come into my vineyard.
I have come to call
all who are waiting for a call.
Go into my vineyard
and pick the harvest.

THE NEW LIFE IS HIDDEN

Why are you afraid?
Can you not see
that I am doing a new thing?
The old order is passing;
it may seem to control events,
as it did at my crucifixion,
but it is being undermined
and split open
by those it considers
weak, powerless, unimportant.

The shoot comes out
after the roots have started
to go down into the soil.
The new life is hidden
but in the breaking down of the seed
and its rooting,
the new life is inevitable
and will soon be revealed.
From its apparent weakness
comes a strength
that can destroy roads
and change a desert
into a garden.

The Church, united in me,
is coming to be
among the humble poor.
Divisions in my body
make no sense to them
in the wilderness
that is the world.
They only see me
crucified for them
and the living water
that flows from my side,
through the working of my Spirit.

Do not be afraid.
I am going to do a new deed
and it is now coming to light.
My Church will be one.
All divisions will be swept away
by the living waters of my sacrifice.

WHERE THE SPIRIT IS PRESENT ...

Where the Spirit is present,
there can all questions be asked
and answered in love.
For where the Spirit of the Lord is,
there is freedom.
The old men of the law
would have been offended
by my questions
if the Spirit had not been with me
in the Temple.

But where the Spirit is present,
there are no divisions,
no standing on status,
no accusations of heresy.
The Spirit teaches all things necessary
to all who ask.
He tells you what to say,
what questions to ask.
All anger and animosity
is banished,
and time and age have no relevance.
The Holy Spirit of the Lord
is food and drink and education
for you all.

I NEED ALL TO HELP

Unity starts helpless and rejected
in a stable.
But the little baby
shines with the light of love,
so that all are drawn to worship
my weakness and my humility.

The centre of the world
is a little child,
weak and helpless in the straw.
How can one
who needs everything to be done for him
rule the nations?

Because I need all to help,
all have a task to do for me.
I am equally grateful
for each service,
and so all feel
equally important and necessary.

For without any one of you,
I should be unable to grow
to my full manhood,
when I will be a glory
to all the peoples of the world,
and all will be all in God.

MOTHER OF UNITY

Mary is the mother
of God's Word,
and like the Word of God
in the scriptures,
Mary's Word
is a source of unity
or a source of division;
we can choose which.
We can use Mary
as a weapon against others,
or we can come to her
as our gentle mother
and meet others
at her knee.

Mary is the channel
by which God came to earth
and we are all
in her debt.
She is the channel
by whose loving care
we can ascend
to her Son.

She is the bridge
between earth and heaven,
our mother,
loving us
and caring for us
and bringing us
to our Brother,
her Son,
our Lord.

I AM ONE GOD THOUGH THREE PERSONS, PERFECT MODEL OF UNITY

You cannot have unity
while you, yourselves, try to negotiate it.
There is only one unity,
new life in the Holy Spirit.
First you must die,
place yourselves completely in my hands,
be buried in the tomb and forgotten by the world.
Then I will raise you up,
and you will come out into the world
and witness to my power and glory.
For you were dead, and now you are alive;
you were lost and forgotten,
and now you are found.

It is only those who have experienced
the darkness of the tomb,
and have shared their passion
with their brothers and sisters,
who will rise as one body;
because in the darkness
they will have come to know
the things that unite them,
and will have supported one another,
sharing the little that they had.
Listen to them and learn from them
for they have been purified,
and so their eyes are opened
and their ears unblocked.

For I am one God though three Persons,
a model for your unity.
Even when I walked on earth,
the Godhead was not divided.
Even in dying on the cross,
there was no separation
of Father, Son and Holy Spirit;
even in the cry from the cross
the Son was not forsaken,
though he felt bereft of all comfort.
And when the Son rose again
it was with the life of the Holy Spirit
sent by the power of the Father.
All three were present,
though hidden beneath the veil
of the risen body,
and all three are present in you
when you are one in me.

ARE YOU LIKE ME?

Nothing could change my love
into hate.
My scourging did not touch
the inner core of my being.
Can you understand
that within myself
I was full of love
for you,
for those who were scourging me
and for those who would crucify me?
On the outside
I was bleeding and mocked;
on the inside
love!
Are you like me?

I see and love
the inner man and woman.
I see past the outside,
from what they seem
to who they are.
No one can hide from me;
I know them as they are
and I love them as they are.

If they respond to my love
then they will wish
to become more lovely to me
because I love them.
I do not condemn them,
I love them
and my love changes them
because they wish to love me
for loving them.

Love is the message
of my scourging,
not resignation to pain,
not acceptance of suffering.
Love changes everything
and is affected by nothing.
Love one another
as I love you
and the world will be changed!

MY MOTHER IS MY PERFECT CREATURE

My mother Mary
was filled with my life.
She is the only one of my creatures
who is filled
with the fullness of God.
For her the kingdom is complete
and God is all in all to her already.
She anticipates your final end,
when you too will be filled
with the fullness of God.
She is your model,
and the only one who is completed.
Imitate her
and be joined in imitating her.
She is my perfect creature
and my mother,
the means by whom
your salvation came into the world,
the source of your unity.

MY FATHER IS TENDER HEARTED

My Father is merciful and righteous;
he is tender hearted.
He protects the simple hearted,
the humble and the meek;
he hears them
when they fall on their knees
to implore his help.

If there had been any other way
he would not have willed
that I endure my passion,
my crucifixion and my death.
He would have saved me
from any part of the humiliation and pain
that was not absolutely necessary.

His words, given through the prophets
and in the lives of his chosen people,
will be exactly fulfilled.
He allows nothing
that will prevent
or reduce
the eternal glory
of his fulfilled creation.
Every step, every meeting, every word
on my way to the cross
was allowed by him
for a purpose.
His purposes are good
and rejoice the heart.

Yes, your troubles,
which are soon over,
train you for the carrying
of the weight of your eternal glory
which is out of proportion to them.
I carried my cross to Calvary
and it was an agonising burden.
But compared to the joy
and the glory of my resurrection,
and to my place at the right hand of my Father
in the overwhelming glory of heaven,
it was as nothing.

And so will your crosses be nothing
by comparison to your glory
when you join me
in the everlasting banquet of heaven.

THE SPIRIT BLOWS WHERE HE WILLS

My Spirit blows where he wills,
and knows no distinctions between persons.
You will know his presence by their fruits.
If they confess that I am Lord
and bring peace and joy through their work,
then my Spirit is in them.
All who are filled with my Spirit are one.

FRIENDS, FOLLOW ME

Are you afraid to follow me to Calvary
in case you are involved
in something you cannot control?
I want friends who follow me
even to the cross itself,
who accept even the most painful changes
in their comfortable lives.
I want each of you
as an individual,
so do not slip back
into the anonymity of your group,
like a timid person in the crowd
by the way of the cross in Jerusalem.

What part would you have played on that day?
Would you have spoken up for me?
Helped me to carry my cross?
Wiped my brow?

I loved everyone along the road,
those who jeered,
those who were afraid,
those who beat me.
I did not judge anyone.
There is no need to be afraid;
I was not recording
who was a friend
and who an enemy.
I loved them all
and longed
for their repentance.
Come, follow me
and do not fear
nor judge.
I am for all.
All are welcome
to follow me.

YOUR REAL NAMES

Call each other
by your real names,
your Christian names.
If you see in your neighbour
an Anglican,
a Baptist,
a Quaker,
then they are separated from you
by a crown of thorns
of your prejudices and preconceptions
that you have placed
on their heads.

They are your brothers and sisters
in my body,
individuals with a name.
You cannot love the man or woman
whom you have crowned
with a label.

You will have unity,
despite your different backgrounds,
if you see each other
as individual people.
You all bring different insights,
different traditions,
to the banquet.
If you were all the same
it would not be a festive meal
but a coming together of robots or slaves.

Welcome your brother or sister
who is different from you,
because each is a unique creation.
Do not crown them with thorns.

REJOICE IN YOUR DIFFERENCES

"And how is it that we hear,
each one of us in his own native language ...
them telling ...
the mighty works of God?"

My Spirit of Love unites.
He makes you all
speak to one another
of the mighty works of God.

He is not concerned
with your different origins;
he wants to make you channels
of God's life in the world.

You need all sorts of men and women
so that somewhere there is someone
who can tell of me
to every person alive on earth.
Rejoice in your differences,
as long as you all confess me
as Lord and Saviour.

You will become me
to all men
through the power
of my Spirit.

In your openness
you will have unity
because all will be
channels of me.

OFFER ME

Judge not
lest you yourselves be judged.
Love takes no pleasure
in other peoples' mistakes.
It is always ready
to excuse,
to trust,
to hope,
and to endure
whatever comes.

Offer me
as your first born leader;
in my name
all are one
and you are joined
as you offer me
in the Eucharist.

As you offer me
to my Father
in the way
that I taught you,
you offer yourselves
in me
and you are one
in me.

I will live in your hearts
and my presence
will fill you
with truth,
and the truth
will make you
one
and free.

I HAVE FORGIVEN YOU

You all left me alone
and deserted me
in my hour of agony.
I know that,
and I have already forgiven you,
if only you will accept
my forgiveness,
and then with me
forget the past
completely.

If I have forgiven you
for your desertion,
why can you not
forgive each other?
Why retain bitter memories
of events which have no meaning
today?
If you accept me as Lord,
then listen to my voice
and obey me.
If I forgive you,
you should forgive
each other.

Each one in the garden
behaved differently;
some ran away,
some used violence,
some followed me
at a safe distance.
And I loved each one of them
as I love each one of you.

I cannot be captured
by one description.
I am all things good
to all good men.
Listen to each other
and learn from each other,
knowing that I love
and speak to everyone
who confesses
that I am their Lord.

And above all
forgive one another
as I have forgiven you.
For if I can forgive you
for your sins to me,
surely you can forgive
each other?
I AM LOVE
WHOM YOU FOLLOW.

BEAUTY IS FROM GOD

Wherever two or three
meet in my name,
I am there in their midst.
It is the humble and meek
who rejoice to come together
in my name,
and I rejoice
to be with them.
The proud and the rich
call on me
but they do not seek me,
and so I do not meet with them.

Beauty is present
when the humble poor gather
to praise my love.
I love to join them
in their humble meetings
where they wait on my words
and rejoice
to be joined together
in love of me.

I do not want
great gatherings
with high dignitaries
and glorious music,
because it is easy
to be carried away
by the glory and the richness
and to forget me,
the carpenter's child,
who is calling you.

Beauty is from God
and the works of great art
that you dedicate to me
are a delight to me
who gave you the gifts
to make them.
But look for me behind them;
do not let your senses
stay on them.
They are a means
to draw you to me;
do not let your hearts
be distracted by them;
come through them
to me.

GIVE PRAISE AT ALL TIMES

Remember to give praise
at all times.
Praise will drive out
despair and hatred and violence.
Praise my Father!
praise me;
praise our Spirit of Love
and you will have peace.

Praise us for our blessings to you
and you will forget
your jealousy
and your covetousness.
For all have gifts,
blessings showered on them,
if only you will look around you
and see what I have done for them.
Praise God in all things
and you will be one.

I CAN SHARE THE PAIN AND THE HAPPINESS WITH YOU

I walked my path to Calvary
so that I might enter
into every part of life.
I experienced every feeling
in my life,
from the highest joy
to the depths of agony.
I have been
in all your experiences.
I can share
the pain and the happiness of life
with each of you.

I am your brother
and your sister.
Come! Share my path with me
so that we may all
be one,
one in following me,
one in sharing
in my redemption
of the world,
one in bringing
the good news
to all
so that God may be
all in all.

MOTHER OF YOUR UNITY

My mother is the mother of your unity.
She anticipated Pentecost
for my Holy Spirit came upon her
at the very beginning
and she agreed to be
the mother of God's Son.
The Church is my Body
and Mary is my mother.
I am One
and she is the mother of one Lord.
In the beginning
all is One,
one Lord,
one Body,
one Church.

Praise my mother,
your mother,
the mother of unity.
Praise her
because the Spirit lived in her
from a time before I was born.
She instructed me
through the Spirit;
she cared for me,
and later for my Church,
in the Spirit;
through my Spirit
I called her to heaven
and there she is
crowned Queen of angels,
the glory of all the saints.

I AM REFLECTED IN YOUR EYES

In the light of the Resurrection
life is too full to think of division.
I am risen from the dead
and I am Lord.
Know me and follow me,
and you must be one
for I am one.
It is no concern to you
whether others describe me
in exactly the same words
as you do.
You can see if they know me
and follow me
because you will see me
reflected in their eyes
and in their actions.
You know the signs;
they speak to you of love.

Go out and tell those
who do not have my light in their eyes,
who have not met me in the garden,
who do not know that I am risen,
that the kingdom of heaven
is in their midst.
If you waste time
seeking to be sure
that it is really me
that others know,
and that they see me clearly,
then many will not have the chance
to hear of me.
Trust me to instruct my friends.
If they are not against you,
then rejoice that you are looking
at the same Lord.

WHO SITS AT MY TABLE?

Those who sit
at my Father's table
are the poor,
the humble,
the weak,
and the pure.
All who have served me
with their whole heart,
and who have had me
as their protector
and their only source
of strength.

I do not ask
to what Church
they belong,
nor whether
they could explain their faith
in absolutely orthodox terms.

What I look for
is a humble and loving heart.
I can enter such a heart
and heal it
and those around it.

My servants
are those
who sit
at my Father's
table
so that
we can serve
them.

MAKE YOURSELF VULNERABLE

How many times have you gloried
in the strength and power of your church
and laughed at the strange, simple behaviour
of others?
It was easy for the Roman soldiers to mock me.
They were safe in the comradeship of their legion,
proud of its solidarity and achievements,
insensitive to the strange people
among whom they found themselves.

And yet Rome is alive today
because of my passion, death and resurrection.
Who remembers the names of those
who crowned me with thorns
or put a purple robe on my shoulders?
I remember them all
and I love them still.
They now know me
and adore me.
My love for them has saved them
and made them one with me.

Do not glory in your power,
but make yourselves vulnerable,
and listening servants
to all your brothers and sisters.
Many call me Lord in strange ways
but all are one
because they follow me.
Recognise those who follow me as their Lord;
join with them and spread my name
to all those who do not yet know me.

For I see into the hearts of all
and I know who calls me Lord
even if they seem to be
far away from me.

Open yourselves to all, as I did,
and trust me to preserve you
through all torments.
They crowned me with thorns
and mocked me,
but I did not allow that
to separate them from my love.

DRY BONES

The peoples of the world are dry bones
waiting for you to breathe life into them.
How can you prophesy if you are not united?
The differences between you
are the stripes of my scourging,
each one more painful than the last.
When will you encourage
and strengthen each other,
rather than quarrel and weaken my words?

For only you, my body, can breathe life
into the dry bones of the peoples.
How long must they wait?
How long will you continue to lay
the stripes of disunity on me?
I have risen and ascended
and I will act through you on earth.
Come together, my people,
and then you can breathe on these dead bones
and make them live again with my life.
For I will send my spirit to flow through you
and they will live.

MY EYES, MY EARS

See as I see;
hear as I hear.
I see the person
I have made.

I hear the songs of gladness,
not of lament.
The loved one
is the one I love.

My love creates
what I love,
no matter if it then turns
away from me.

You are yourself,
as I made you,
singing songs of gladness
as I taught you.

For I see
and hear you
as I keep you
and sustain you.

Search for the one
I make in others,
and they will respond
to the one I make in you.

LISTEN TO EACH OTHER

Your eyes have seen your salvation
which has been prepared
in the presence of all peoples.
I call to all men,
not to some exclusive group alone.
How do you know when talking to a friend
that you both know the same third person?
You can be certain that your descriptions
will be different.

You know that you are referring
to the same person
because you trust each other,
and by listening
you can see that your friend's description
could fit.
He has given you a new insight
and you have gained in understanding.

Listen to each other.
If you can see that what is said could be true,
then trust each other
and accept what is said
even if it is new and strange.
Only reject
anything that contradicts
what you know to be true
about me.

I am the light of revelation
to all people.
I may not appear as you would expect.
I have been offered to my Father
and my offering
has brought salvation
to all men.
Join hands with your fellows
and bless my name,
for I have redeemed you all
from sin and everlasting death.

MY LOVE HAS NO CONDITIONS

How could the Creator,
the God who made
all that is,
send his Son,
his very Word,
co-substantial
and co-eternal,
to be scourged
and mocked
and crucified?

How did those creatures,
who inflicted
torments on the Lord,
survive their attack
on God himself?

Do not all
who look on his face
perish?
And do not those
who hear his voice
stand transfixed
with fear?

Would not
the very wood of the crown
cease to be
as it touched
his forehead?
Would not the whips
turn back
as they approached
his back?

What God
would allow
such things
to be done to him
by his own creatures?

My love
is everlasting
and without limit.
You can have
no idea of the depths,
or the height
or the breadth
of the love
of God.
Taste and see
how precious
is the love
of your Lord.

You have been allowed
to tear my body
because my love
is unconditional.
I wear
my crown of thorns
to implore you
to turn back to me
and to each other
in love,
my love.

WHO STANDS WITH ME?

Do you stand with me at my arrest,
or do you run away?
I do not need protection,
but your love.
My Father's will is that I submit.
Will you submit with me?
Will you accept the pain
and the scorning?
Be rejected and imprisoned?

Unity comes through passion,
not through calm reasoning.
There is no reason for disunity;
its causes lie in pride and emotion,
in memories of injustice and intolerance.
It can only be healed by forgiveness,
and by submission in love.

Pray and make yourselves vulnerable
as I did.
Submit to the judgements
of those who are in authority.
Resistance cannot enter their hearts,
but love can.
Resistance only confirms their actions,
but submission convicts them
and heals them.

MARKS OF LOVE

The disciples going to Emmaus were led there by my words.
I showed them the truth of the scriptures
and my message found a home in their hearts;
but they recognised me in the breaking of bread.
For as I took the bread and broke it,
they looked at my hands,
and they saw the marks of the nails,
and they knew they were forgiven.

I carry the wounds of my passion
so that all can see
that I accepted them in love for you.
I would not show them if I had not forgiven you
for all the pain that I endured.
I make no attempt to hide my wounds,
but show them as marks
of my forgiveness and love.
You must do the same,
forgiving one another
as soon as any quarrel begins.

I am your Lord,
and if you acknowledge me as Lord,
you must do my will.
My will is that my peace
should reign in your hearts,
because it was for this
that you were called together
as parts of my body.

Always be thankful,
and encourage each other to give thanks to me
for my dying and for my rising again,
by which you have peace and everlasting life
in the body of your Risen Lord.

PRIDE IS OPAQUE

When you meet your brethren
do their hearts leap for joy
as Elisabeth's did
at the coming of my mother?
Do they know that you carry within you
my living presence?
Do you sense my presence in them?
Every coming together should be
an occasion for rejoicing
at the living presence of your Lord within you.

And take note
that my mother came to Elisabeth.
The mother of God came to her cousin
and so you should go
to your brothers and sisters
and not expect them to come to you.
The greatest among you is the servant of all,
for I am the suffering servant
who offered up his life for all.

You will have unity
when the world sees you
as imitators of my mother
who did not stand on her status
but came humbly to her cousin Elisabeth.
For humility is transparent to my presence,
and pride is opaque.

If you are humble
my life will shine out through you;
but if you are proud
your pride will hide my presence.

DO NOT CLING TO YOUR PAST

All I carried on my way to Calvary
was a crown of thorns
and a heavy crosspiece of wood;
With these I bought the salvation of the world.
Why do you store up so many possessions,
your dogmas, your rituals and your buildings?
All that is needed
is my cross,
and the empty tomb.

Your riches divide you,
the way of the cross unites you.
Sell all that you have and follow me.
Do not cling to your sacred property,
but be prepared to give it up
to join those following me
on my way to Calvary.

And you will find your hearts lighter
and your step firmer
if you only carry your cross
and wear your crown of thorns,
rather than the weight
of your traditions
and your performances.
Follow me.

COME INTO MY PRESENCE

Come into my presence
with thanksgiving and praise;
come to my throne in the stable.
I, your Lord, am lying in a manger
with animals round my cradle.
I begin my life on earth
in the lowest place.

I did not want
to be born in a palace.
Men and women
would hesitate to approach me there;
only the rich and privileged
would see a royal infant.

I was born in a stable
open to anyone who cared to enter,
with no comforts, no barriers,
nothing to make anyone feel inferior,
or afraid.
Come to my cradle;
you must seek me there
if you are to have unity.

For all must kneel in praise
on the straw around me,
and all must sing of my glory
surrounded by the smells and sounds
of the world;
all must brave the darkness
and the narrowness of the entrance,
trusting in my grace as they enter,
for they cannot see the glory
which lies within.

All are welcome
as long as they kneel to enter
and discard their pride.
All are invited
who will praise God for his love
in entering his world
so humbly,
and not with overwhelming power.

For my power is shown in weakness,
and my love surrounds you
when you are in darkness
or cast down with sorrow.
I made you to live with me in love
and to praise me
for my free gift of myself to you.
Come to the stable,
and be one with your humble Lord
who lives with you in love.

THE DARKNESS OF NO-PEACE

Go out into the whole world
and proclaim the good news to all creation.
I am with you until the end of time.
Do not only talk about me,
but DO my message of peace.
To dress the wounds of the world without love
does not spread my message.
If you do not speak peace
to your brothers and sisters,
how can the world see that your words
are my words,
bringing life to all who live
in the darkness of death
and of no-peace?

ACCEPT YOUR PARENTAGE

Your mother, Mary, is queen of heaven.
You are all one family
through her Son's offering of himself.
I, the Lord God,
asked her to be my mother,
and made my plans
for the redemption
of all creation
dependent on her will.
If you ask her
to be your mother
she will be the means
of unity among you.

You are the family of God.
Accept your parentage;
be proud of your lineage;
praise God for incorporating you
into his family,
into his living presence.

REMOVE THE NAILS
SO I CAN COME DOWN

I can only come down from the cross
if you remove the nails
that you have hammered in.
And the pulling out will be as painful
as the hammering in.
For the nails are the injustices
you have inflicted on the poor,
and the pulling out is the restitution
that you must make to them.

You are all one body, my body;
and you are all crucified with me
by the injustices and sorrows of the world.
I am nailed to the cross in my poor
but my coming down
will be an agony for the rich.

But if you are all laid with me
in my mother's arms,
so that your wounds may be bathed by her tears,
then with me you will rise remade.
And in that time
no one will need to teach anyone;
you will all know me,
the least no less than the greatest,
since I will forgive your iniquity
and never call your sins to mind.

LISTEN TO MY WORDS

Speak the words
that my Spirit gives you,
in truth to one another.
For the words of my Spirit
bring peace to the hearts
of all who hear them.
I give joy and peace
by my words
to all who trust me;
and I want them
to speak my words to others
so that the world may be filled
with my love.

The words of Simeon,
my words,
live for ever,
for he spoke truth
to Mary and Joseph
in love,
and brought joy and peace
to their hearts.
The words of Anna
brought joy to all
who heard them.
Listen to my words
and speak of them
to all you meet.
For in my words
is unity and peace.
– says the Lord.

MY CROWN OF THORNS UNITES YOU

My crown of thorns unites you
for there can be no jealousy
in wearing it.
It has no earthly value
and wounds those who bear it.
You are united by love,
and love involves passion.
You are separated by wealth and power
which bring jealousy and possessiveness.

You have freedom as sons of God
through my blood;
your sins are forgiven
through my blood,
the agony in the garden,
the scourging,
the crown of thorns
and the crucifixion.
Will you follow me
and offer your blood for others,
your pain,
your sacrifice
of things you hold dear,
and of yourself?

Replace your crown of pride
with a crown of thorns,
and you will be one
in my blood,
and you will be free.

CHILDREN OF THE PROMISE

A woman screams out in labour
and her pains are worst
just before her baby is born.
The child of the promise
is born of those who had despaired
of having children,
but who believed
that all things are possible
with God.

When your pains are worst
and your despair deepest,
look for me to be among you;
expect me to come again.
For within my faithful remnant,
my bride who despairs of fruitfulness,
I will be born
and will bring the world to new life,
my kingdom on earth.

Praise me
in the agony of your labour.
Cry out with joy
as the pain grows fiercer,
for you know
that I have promised you salvation
and that I will not come again
unless you labour
to bring me to birth.

And who are
the people of the promise?
They are my people Israel,
long separated from me;
and you are my Benjamin,
born from Israel out of time,
when it seemed that Israel,
my bride,
was barren and defeated.

You are incorporated in my people,
but Israel is your older brother
to whom you must pay
due honour.
Embrace him,
for you are both
children of the promise,
but his is the inheritance
of the older son.

TURN THE OTHER CHEEK

Submit to the pain
of mockery and persecution,
and let nothing change your love
for those who provoke you.
If you live by the Spirit,
the fruit of the Spirit
must shine out in your life:
love, joy, peace, patience,
kindness, goodness, faithfulness,
gentleness and self-control.

If all love you,
there is little difficulty
in showing the fruit of the Spirit;
even those who live by the world
do that.
But when you are scourged,
mocked, persecuted,
then the fruit of the Spirit
shining through your lives
is a message of love and wonder
to the world.

If your brother strikes you,
turn the other cheek
and forgive him,
for he knows not what he does.
If your sister provokes you
by false argument,
seek to answer her with patience,
for she is mistaken.
Love those who persecute and hate you
if you will have unity,
for only thus
will they recognise me
in your lives
and in your words.

I CANNOT LIE

Your unity must be found in my Word.
Nothing that contradicts my words can be from me
Discard it immediately.

Listen to your brothers and sisters
and ask questions of them,
as I did of the doctors of the law.
I, the Son of God,
the very Word of God,
listened to the doctors
and found that their knowledge
increased my understanding.
And when my questions
caused them to dispute among themselves,
they were taught by their own arguments
and not by my correction.

Listen in love
and oppose all that contradicts my words.
For I cannot lie,
nor speak words that are not fulfilled.
In my words you will have unity
if you listen to one another
in love.

DISCERNMENT

Offer the word in the temple
and hear whether those who have waited for it
recognise it as the word of God.
Otherwise you will not have unity.
And submit to the decision of the elders.

COME CLOSER INTO MY LIGHT

Listen,
for in the light of my rising
you can see the faces
of your brothers and sisters.
Every face turned towards me
grows brighter
and is never ashamed.
If you look at me,
malice will be banished from your tongue,
deceitful conversation from your lips;
because all your words will be praise,
and in praise
there can be no condemnation
nor division.

So look at me
and let your faces shine
in the light of my Resurrection.
You will be drawn closer to me,
and so closer to each other.
A time will come
when you will stretch out
and link hands with your neighbours
so that you can dance for joy
round your risen Lord.

TRAVEL TOGETHER IN A BODY

You will need all your strength
to reach Calvary.
You cannot afford to waste any energy
on quarrels or disputes.
For you are all heirs
to the promises made to Israel,
and joined with Israel
in one body,
and you share together
in my mission and power.

Travel together in a body,
and welcome all
who acknowledge me as Lord
and who long for the coming of my kingdom.
The way is hard,
but joyful if you travel as one body,
encouraging each other
and sharing the gifts
that I have given you.

I am the Lord of all
and I lead you
to the glory of my Father's kingdom
by a road of terrible love,
a love that spends everything for others
but is refreshed and renewed
every time that it is spent,
so that joy and peace are
ever in your hearts.

YOU WILL BE ONE IN HEAVEN

In the glory of Heaven
you will have eyes only for God,
and the light that is God
will flood your whole being,
whether from inside or outside you will not know.
In that light there can be no divisions,
and the light of your shining
will be the presence of God in you.

You will be one in Heaven
so why maintain divisions on earth?
What do they achieve or signify?
You cannot take them with you,
and you will not be able to understand
why you maintained them
when you see how unimaginably different
the reality of God is
in comparison to your attempts to define him.

Mary, my mother, will smile on you,
filling your hearts with love for her.
And you will wonder how you have made someone
so lovely, so pure, so perfect
a cause of scandal and mockery between you.
You will be proud to have her as your Queen
as you join with her in the hymns of praise
that are the everlasting joy of Heaven.

You pray to my Father that his kingdom may come
on earth as it is in Heaven.
Do you know what you pray for?
His kingdom knows no divisions,
no denominations, no sects.
His kingdom is a kingdom of everlasting praise,
heartfelt praise of his love,
his faithfulness,
his mercy and his creative power.

Pray for the kingdom to come on earth,
and make it come sooner
by embracing your brothers and sisters now,
as you will embrace them for ever
in love in Heaven.

A HOLY NATION SET APART

Nothing can be achieved without work.
"With suffering and the sweat of your brow
you will get your food from the earth."
Nothing of value can be attained
without pain and hard work.
Your salvation was no exception
for it cost me the agony of my passion,
my crowning with thorns and my death.
I sweated blood
in the work of your redemption.

You will only have unity
through pain and hard work.
There are so many walls to be broken down,
so many crowns of gold to be melted
and replaced by the thorns of humility.
Follow me
and accept the agony of the path to unity
on which you will have to give up
so many treasures of your past,
in order to come to the one cross
and to be joined to me in the sight of all nations,
a holy nation set apart.

COMPETITION IN SERVICE

There is no division in love,
and my cross is the final expression of love;
that one man should give his life
in agony for all men and women.
And you should do likewise
if you are asked to do so.
If all my consecrated nation,
all of my kingdom of priests,
are ready to follow me,
even to death on a cross,
from where do your divisions come?

If all try to serve each other,
then there will be competition in service
and not in power,
nor superiority in understanding.
In my agony I forgave those who crucified me,
I healed the loving thief,
I gave my mother to you all.
There were neither arguments nor division
in my dying,
but a continuous offering of myself to you.

So love one another
even to giving your lives for another,
and there will be no disunity among you.

ACCEPT INSECURITY

You are one in the Spirit,
and you do not acknowledge
that Spirit,
preferring
to divide
my body
for your own
security.
Think of my mother,
the mother of your unity.

She accepted insecurity,
the mockery of those round her
because
to bear a child before marriage
made her an object
of contempt
of those who trusted
in their own righteousness
and judged
their neighbours harshly.

Accept the hostility
and scorn of the world
while you accept
my Spirit
who unites you.
Seek me
and I will come
with my Father and the Spirit
who joins us
in love;
and we
will make our home
in you
as we made our home in Mary,
the mother of your unity.

LIFT UP YOUR EYES

If you are tired,
lift up your eyes
and see my holy mountains.
You are on your way
to the new Jerusalem
with a great company,
a mighty nation,
a people set apart
who acknowledge me,
your God,
as King.

Do not allow
the pressures of the world
to overcome you.
You are mine.
I called you by your names
when I redeemed you.
Satan will try to conquer you
as he tried to conquer me,
but if you call on me,
your King,
he cannot prevail.

Peace will be there
everlastingly
when you come to the mountains
of the new Israel.
Peace is in your hearts
if you make them temples
of the living God.
Peace will be in your hearts
but it can never reign in the world
until I come again.
Pray for my kingdom to come,
the new Jerusalem,
if you would have peace.

Pray that all things
are directed towards
the coming of the kingdom
and you will have peace soon.
Do not seek to preserve
your own comfort and idleness,
for that delays
the coming of the kingdom.

For my kingdom comes first
to the poor and the humble,
not to the rich and the powerful.
I am the Lord,
your God and King,
and I will rule you
by my laws,
which are just and true
and not like the world's laws.

Welcome me as your king,
and the new kingdom of the humble
will be a land of peace.

SEEK THOSE WHO LOVE MY WORDS

Who are the pharisees today?
Who will oppose them for me,
because they put guilt
where I want loving hearts,
and they drive men away from my table?

Where can you go
to drink of my law,
the law of love?
My mother and Joseph found me
in my Father's house,
listening to the doctors of the law
and asking them questions.
I felt at home,
and I had no fear of those old men
because they loved my Father's words
and they loved all those
who sought to understand them.

So seek those who love my words
and who share them with you
in humility.
For it is not by words alone
that you will be saved,
but also by the love
that flows from the hearts of those
who have heard my words
and then have kept them in their hearts,
treasuring them and pondering over them.

Seek loving hearts,
not magnificent words.
I am to be found most easily
among the humble and the poor,
not among the princes of the world.
For the poor have few garments
to hide their real selves,
and the humble do not pretend
to be greater than they are.
Seek those who know me
and have welcomed me into their hearts,
rather than those who know much about me.

You are united by love,
my love for you
and your love returned for mine,
not by your knowledge.

I CAN DO NO MORE TO PERSUADE YOU

I can allow you
to tear my body apart
as I allowed the soldiers
to crucify me on Calvary.
And you still mock me
as they did,
because I do not save myself.

Why did I not come down from the cross?
Why do I not heal my divided body?
It is because I love you, my people;
I respect your freedom.
You have eaten of the tree
of the knowledge of good and evil,
and now you have the right to choose for yourself
what you will do.

I will only show you the way
to everlasting life.
I will not force you to march along it
like a band of slaves
chained together by my laws.

Whatsoever you ask in my name
will be granted.
But you must ask in faith,
believing me to be the Son of God
and your loving Lord.
My death on the cross is a sign
of my unconditional love;
if you believe in my love,
then you will not ask for any more proof.

You are not children
to be told what to do
and then punished for disobedience;
you are my brothers and sisters,
I have called you friends.
If you are my friends,
you should be joined to one another
through your friendship with me.
It is because you do not believe in your hearts
that I am the Son of God
that you are divided.

If you truly believe
that I am your Lord,
then you will be united
in praise and worship of me.
I can do nothing more
to give you the proof that you ask for;
I can do no more than to die for you
and if that does not persuade you of my love,
no act of miraculous power
will do so either.

COME! SET ASIDE YOUR DIFFERENCES

When I intervene in the world,
I come quickly and act decisively,
and the course of history is changed.
I came as a child,
and grew up to be a man;
then in three short years,
I brought good news to the poor,
was crucified and rose again,
and the world was a different place.

And so it will be now;
three years will pass,*
and you will not recognise your world,
but you will kneel before my majesty once more.
Do not be afraid, my people;
rejoice that I am intervening in history again
to cleanse the world
from the consequences of sin.

I put down the mighty
from their positions of power,
and I exalt the humble and poor.
You can never anticipate how I will act,
because I do something new every day,
and you do not see the world as I see it.
I am not limited by what has gone before.
You must forget your past greatness
and humble yourselves.

Come with your gifts to the stable
and give them to the little child.
In your long separation from one another
each one of you has perfected
your understanding of one part of my Good News.
Now is the time to bring them all together:
the gold of knowledge and authority,
the incense of praise and worship,
and the myrrh of suffering and self-denial.
Bring your gifts to the stable
and lay them at my feet and do me homage.

Come! Set aside your differences
and unite in worship of me,
so that I may grow among you
and bring all things to their consummation in me.

Ed. note. These words were received in prayer on 17th August, 1990.

Valedictory

THE MEADOWS OF ADORATION

Oh my people! What are you doing to me:
I came as an innocent child,
to convict the world with my innocence
and my humility,
to judge the poor with tenderness
and the miserable with fairness and affirmation.

And you have set yourselves up
as judges over the people.
You utter blasphemies
against the works of my breath.
You murder and enslave the innocent and poor;
you divide my people for your own glory.

Come back to me, my people;
come back to the stable and the little child.
Let me lead you in paths of peace as one flock,
following the Lamb of God
into the everlasting sheepfold,
where no unjust judges,
no murderers,
no thieves
ever come,
and where all are pastured
in the meadows of adoration.

Richard died on 30th March 1993.

"Surely goodness and mercy
shall follow me all the days of my life,
and I shall dwell in the house of the Lord forever."
Psalm 23

Postscript

For several years before he died at the age of 59, Richard had been asked by our many friends in Renewal to publish the 'prophetic words' which the Lord spoke into his heart during his times of prayer. These same friends have been a great support to me since he died, and I want to express my thanks to them, and to all my children, for the help they have given me to get through the last two years.

Above all I want to thank Ron Nicholls. Richard always relied heavily on his discernment and wise counsel, and I am very happy that I have been able to do so myself in the compiling and editing of this little book.

The title "The Desire of My Heart" refers to Our Lord's prayer in Ch. 17 of St. John's Gospel, a prayer with which Richard identified completely, being more saddened by Christian disunity than by anything else: *'Father, may they all be one ...'*

E.K.H.

If you have been inspired by these 'Words' from the Lord
you may like to receive further information, book lists,
and details of the magazine "Good News" from the
Catholic Charismatic Renewal Centre, Allen Hall,
28 Beaufort Street, London SW3 5AA
Telephone: 0171-352 5298 or 0171-352 5311
Fax: 0171-351 4486